HOW ♥ TO LOVE

For everyone I've ever had a crush on.

Especially those who had a crush on me too.

Especially especially Ruby, my biggest crush.

First US edition 2023

Library of Congress Catalog Card Number 2022922799
ISBN 978-1-5362-1788-9

23 24 25 26 27 28 APS 10 9 8 7 6 5 4 3 2 1

Printed in Humen, Dongguan, China

This book was typeset in WB Alex Norris.
The illustrations were created digitally.

Walker Books US
a division of
Candlewick Press
99 Dover Street
Somerville, Massachusetts 02144

www.walkerbooksus.com

HOW to LOVE

A GUIDE TO FEELINGS & RELATIONSHIPS FOR EVERYONE

alex norris

WALKER BOOKS

CONTENTS

TOGETHER:
QUESTIONS ABOUT BEING IN A RELATIONSHIP

EVER AFTER:
QUESTIONS ABOUT WHAT COMES NEXT

INTROD

UCTION

you

Here you are, floating
blissfully through the
void of lovelessness.

Then you
see someone

someone beautiful
and fascinating

and compellingly
aloof.

Suddenly:

feelings.

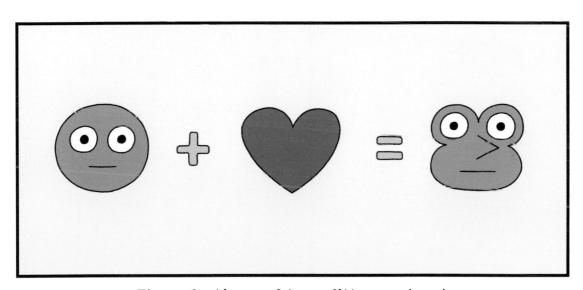

These feelings of love fill your head

and transform you

into something intense
and desperate.

Your Beloved
runs away

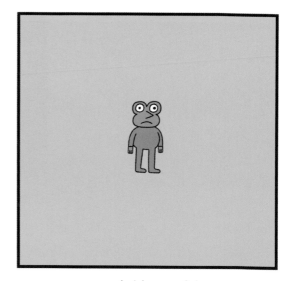

and the void
feels very empty.

You search for help, and find a handy guide.

It does not
run away.

You hold it in
your hands

and love it forever.

WHAT IS THIS BOOK?

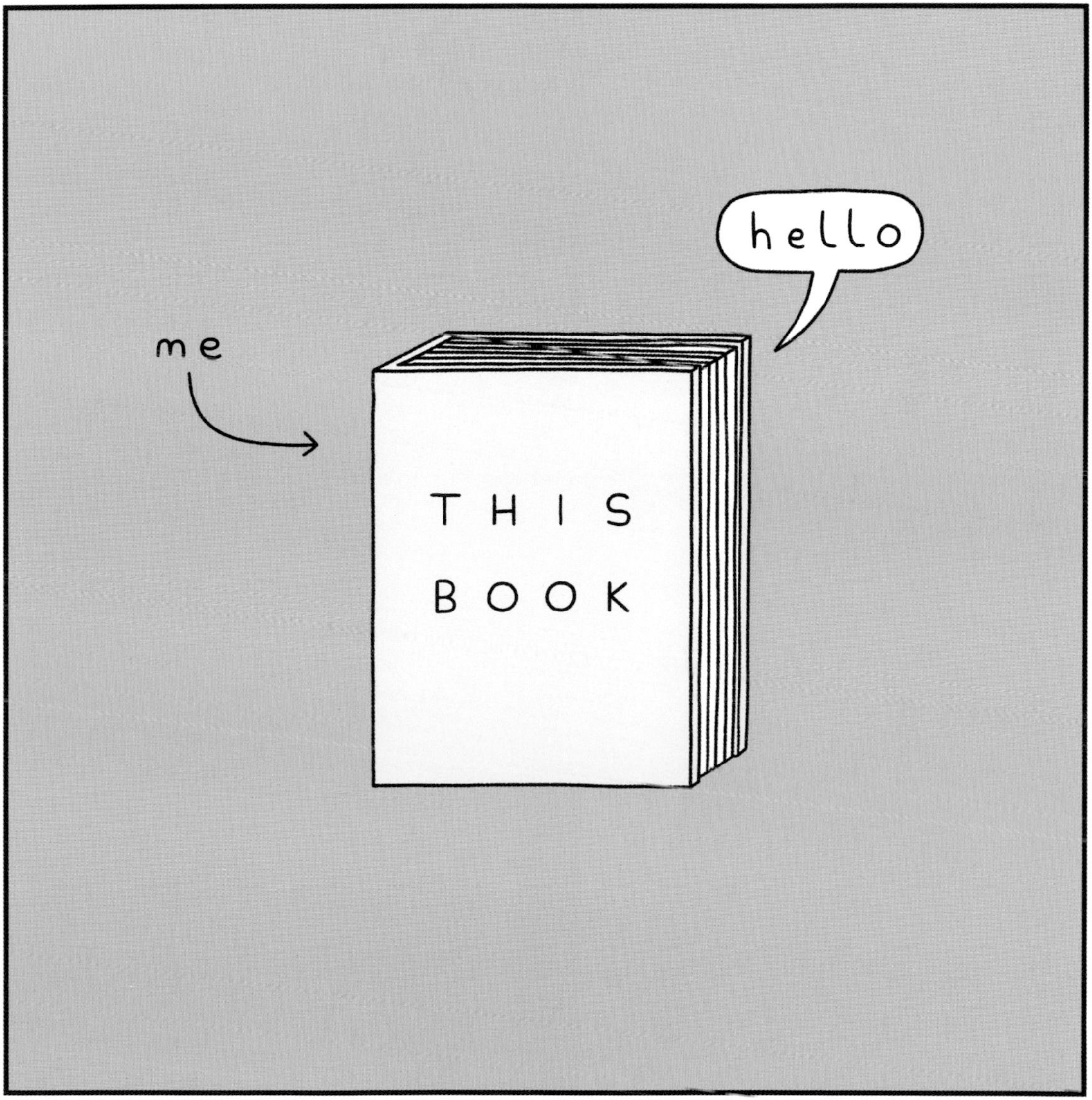

hello
me
THIS
BOOK

This book might seem very
normal on the surface

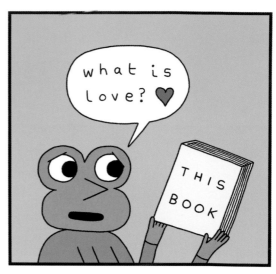

but like in any relationship

once you get to know it, you'll realize
this book is actually quite weird.

You may think you need to
be "normal" to be loved.

Maybe you are looking for a
book that will help you fit in

tell you the rules of love

and how to follow them.

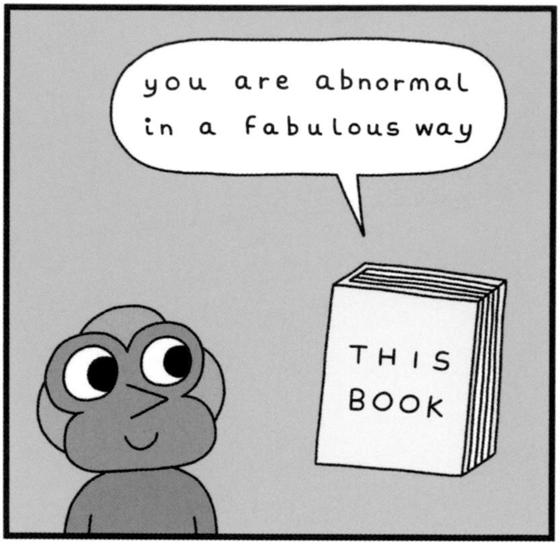
you are abnormal in a fabulous way
THIS BOOK

When it comes to love, we are surrounded by rules and conventions.

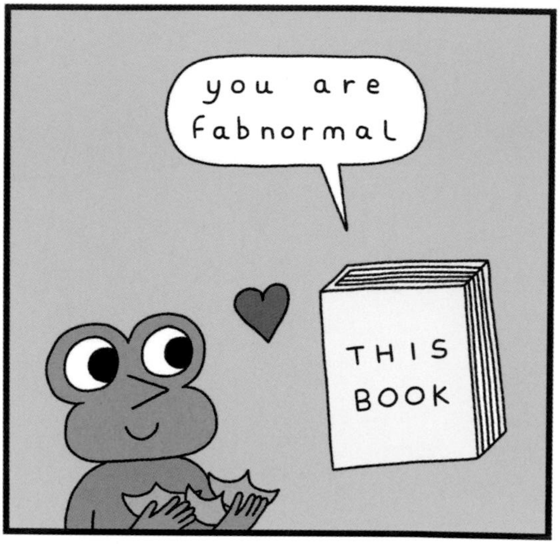
you are fabnormal
THIS BOOK

This book will show you how absurd these conventions can be

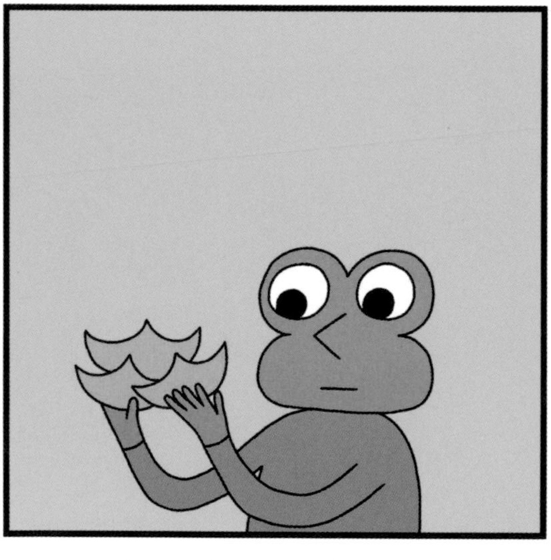

and explore other ways of doing things

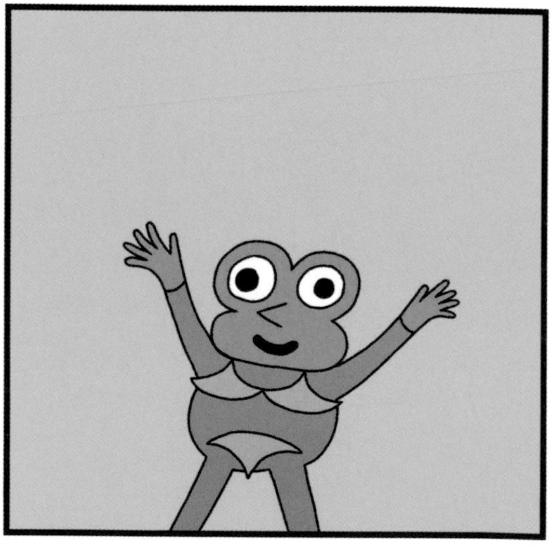

that might better suit YOU.

The ideas and metaphors
in this book are not
definitive answers

but they may help you to
see love in new ways

keep you questioning

and exploring

so you can be free to build
your own approach to love.

ALL BY

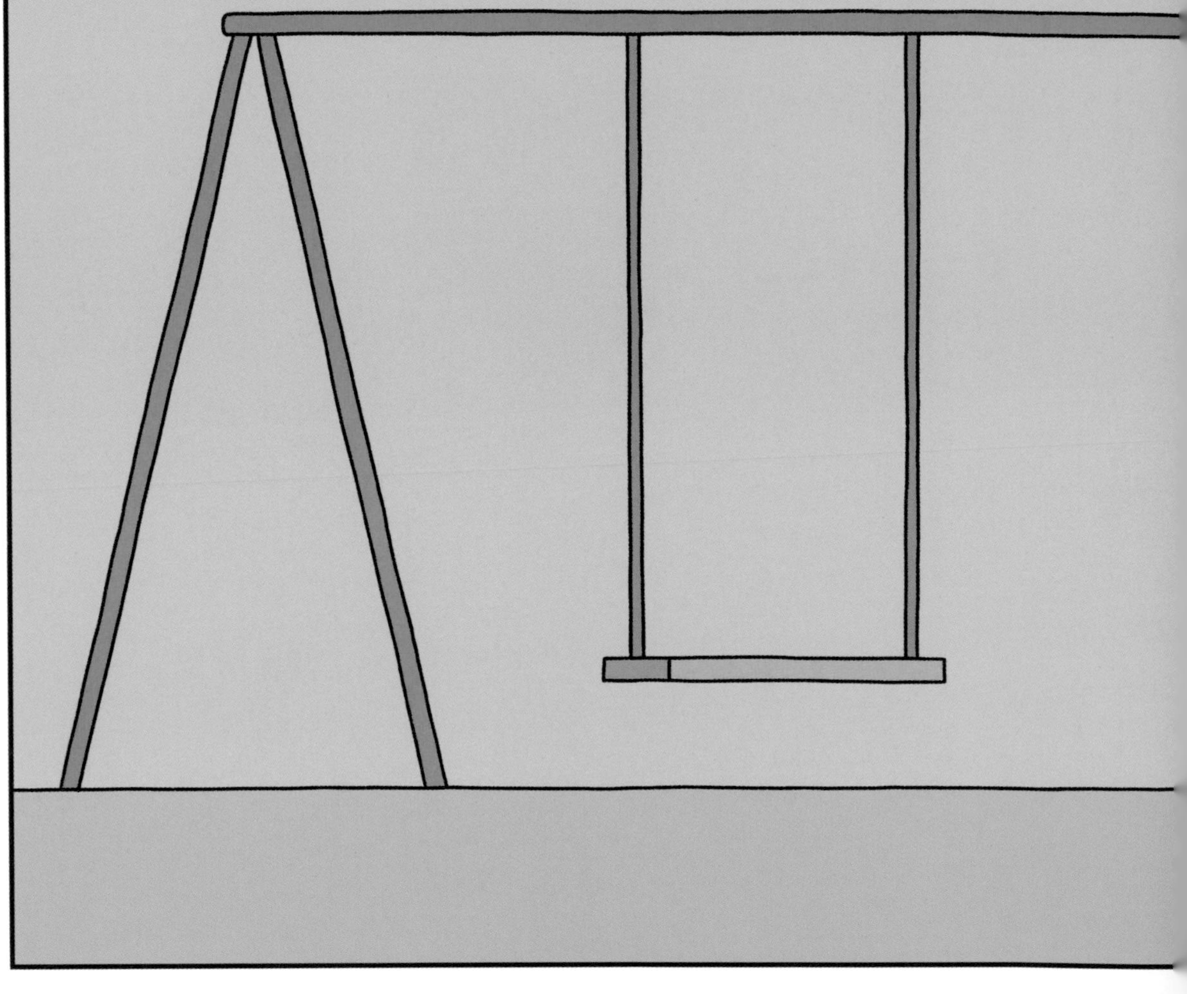

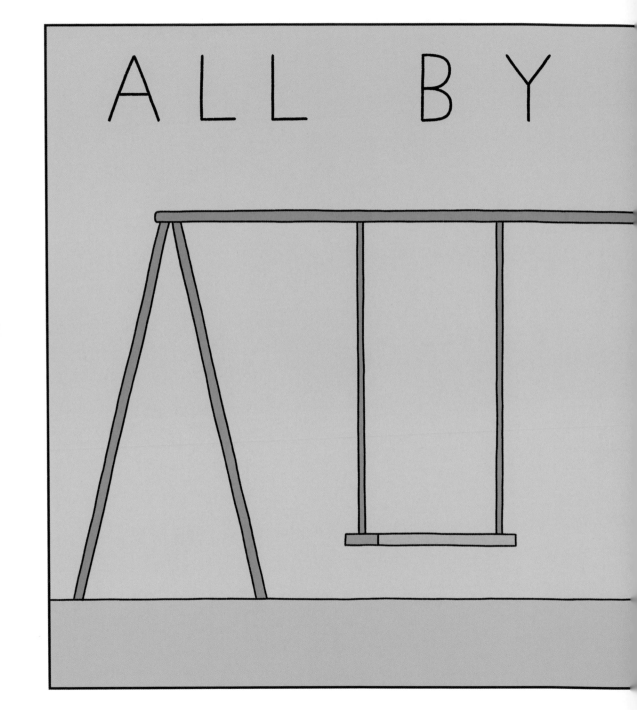

MYSELF

QUESTIONS ABOUT BEING SINGLE

DO I NEED LOVE?

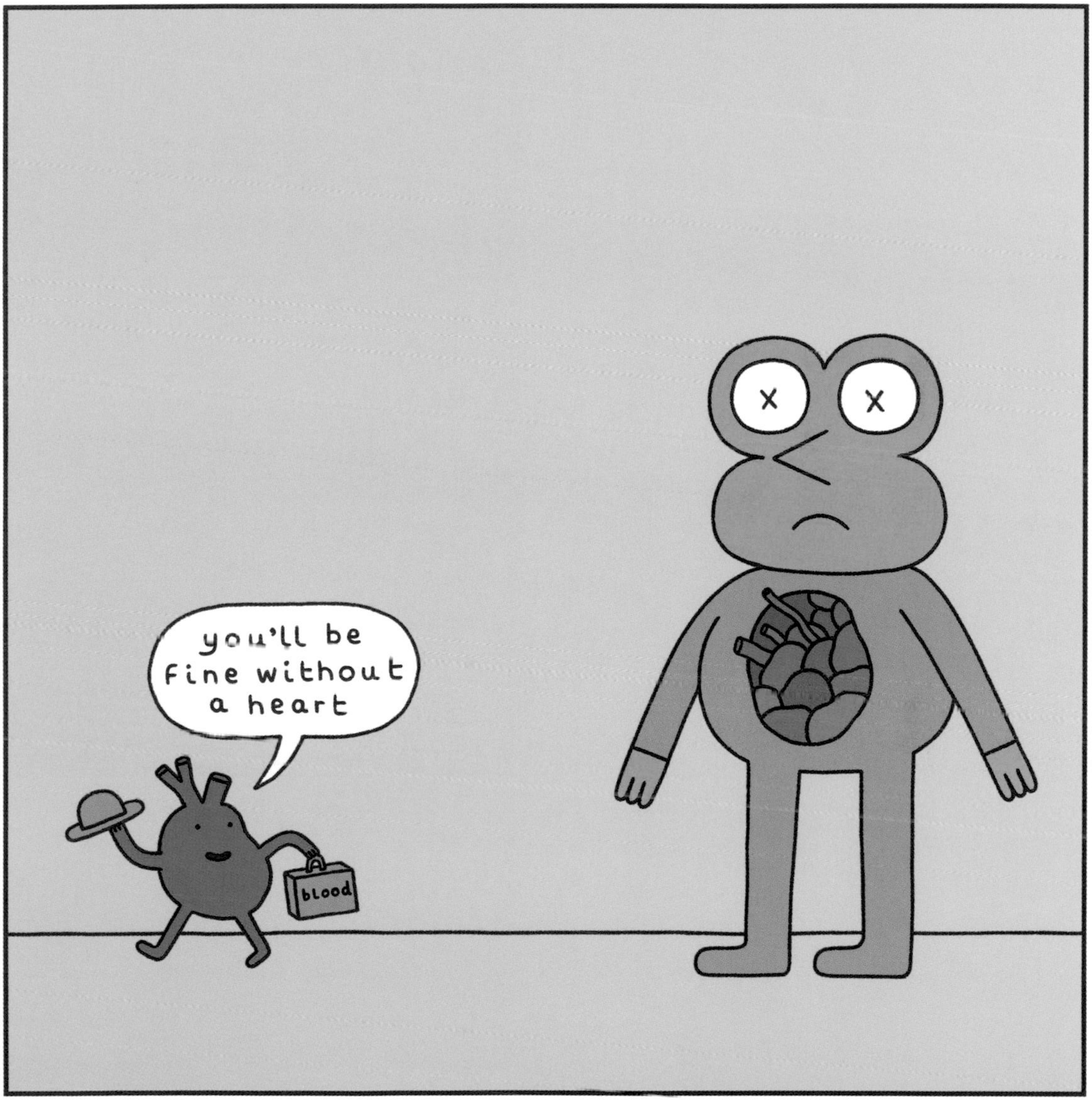
you'll be fine without a heart
blood

We all need love to
feel truly whole

but you don't always need
to find it in someone else.

Sometimes the best
place to find love

is in the mirror.

Self-love doesn't have
to be narcissistic.

It doesn't have to be big
and grand and unwavering.

It can be as simple

as teaming up with yourself.

If you want someone who has
the same needs, interests,
and aspirations as you

someone who understands
you, who you can spend
a lot of time with

and can offer you kindness,
patience, and support

you will find yourself
very lovable.

Loving yourself means you
will have more in common
with those who love you.

Self-love can teach you
how to accept love

and how to give
love to others.

But it is also much easier
to be by yourself

once you learn to give
yourself the love you need.

WHAT IF I LIKE BEING SINGLE?

You don't need to pursue
traditional romance

to have a wonderful life

filled with intensity, intimacy, comfort, love, joy, and passion.

But even if you are
having a perfectly lovely
time being single

people may pressure
you to change.

They assume you must
be unhappy and lonely

without a traditional
romantic relationship.

Everyone has different types of relationships
that are important to them:

friends, family,
companions, pets

colleagues, carers,
teammates, allies

heroes, mentors, neighbors, acquaintances, rivals.

The truth is you are not "single" at all.

Traditional romance may fit into your life

but it also might not.

How you arrange
things is up to you.

WHAT IF I FEEL LONELY?

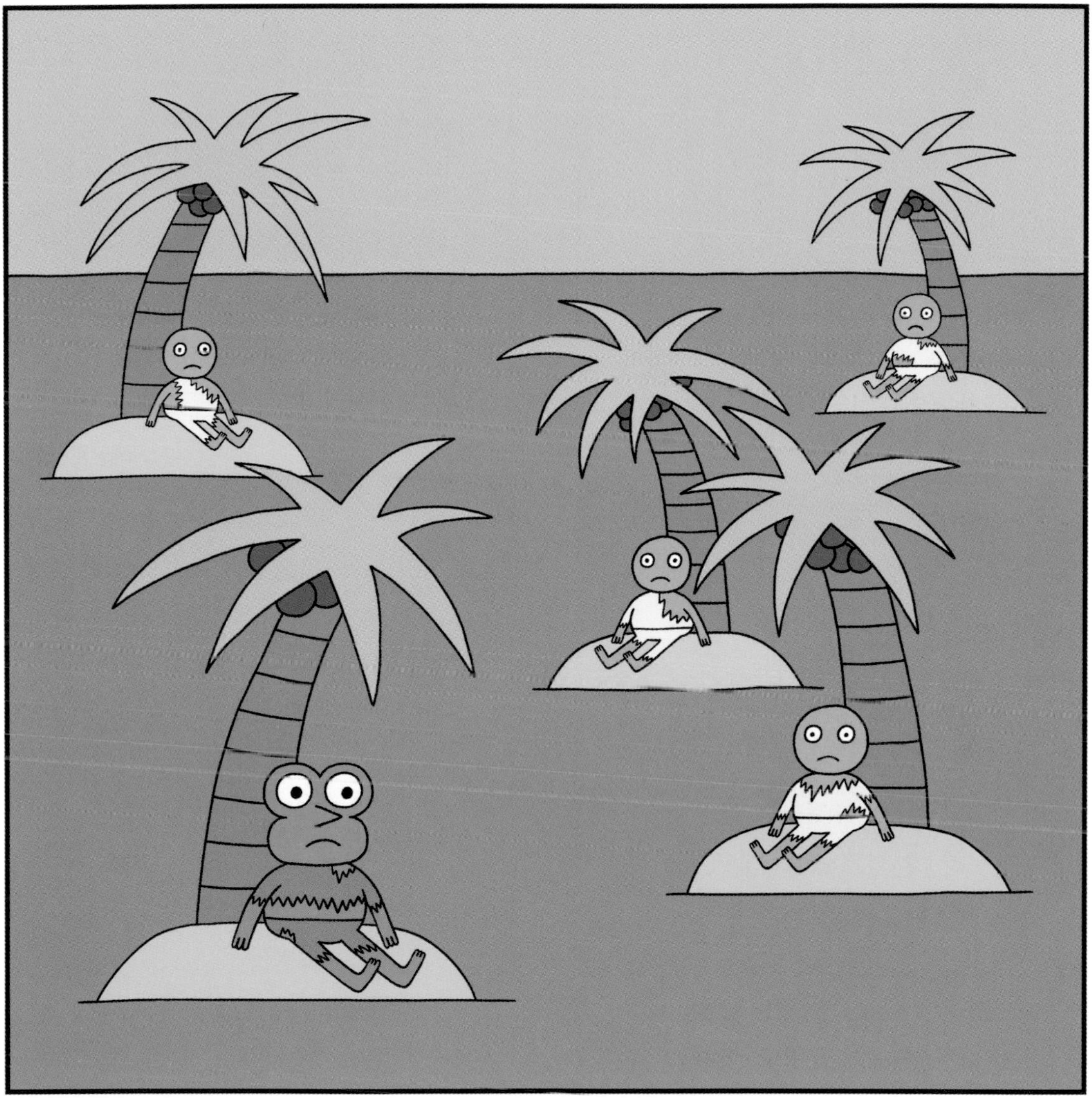

You may be reading this book about love because you feel lonely

like Rapunzel in her tower, waiting for someone to come along.

Loneliness isn't just a lack of company.

It can feel like a wall between you and the world.

You can be lonely at a party
surrounded by friends.

You can be lonely in
a relationship.

People may be there

but you don't feel
the connection.

The first thing to do is
admit that you feel lonely.

An intense romance might
seem like a good solution

but it is unlikely to
bring you comfort

if it demands too much
intimacy too quickly.

But by looking inward

and taking steps to feel more grounded

your loneliness will feel less powerful.

You will be more able to make small connections

and feel part of the world.

WHO SHOULD I LOVE?

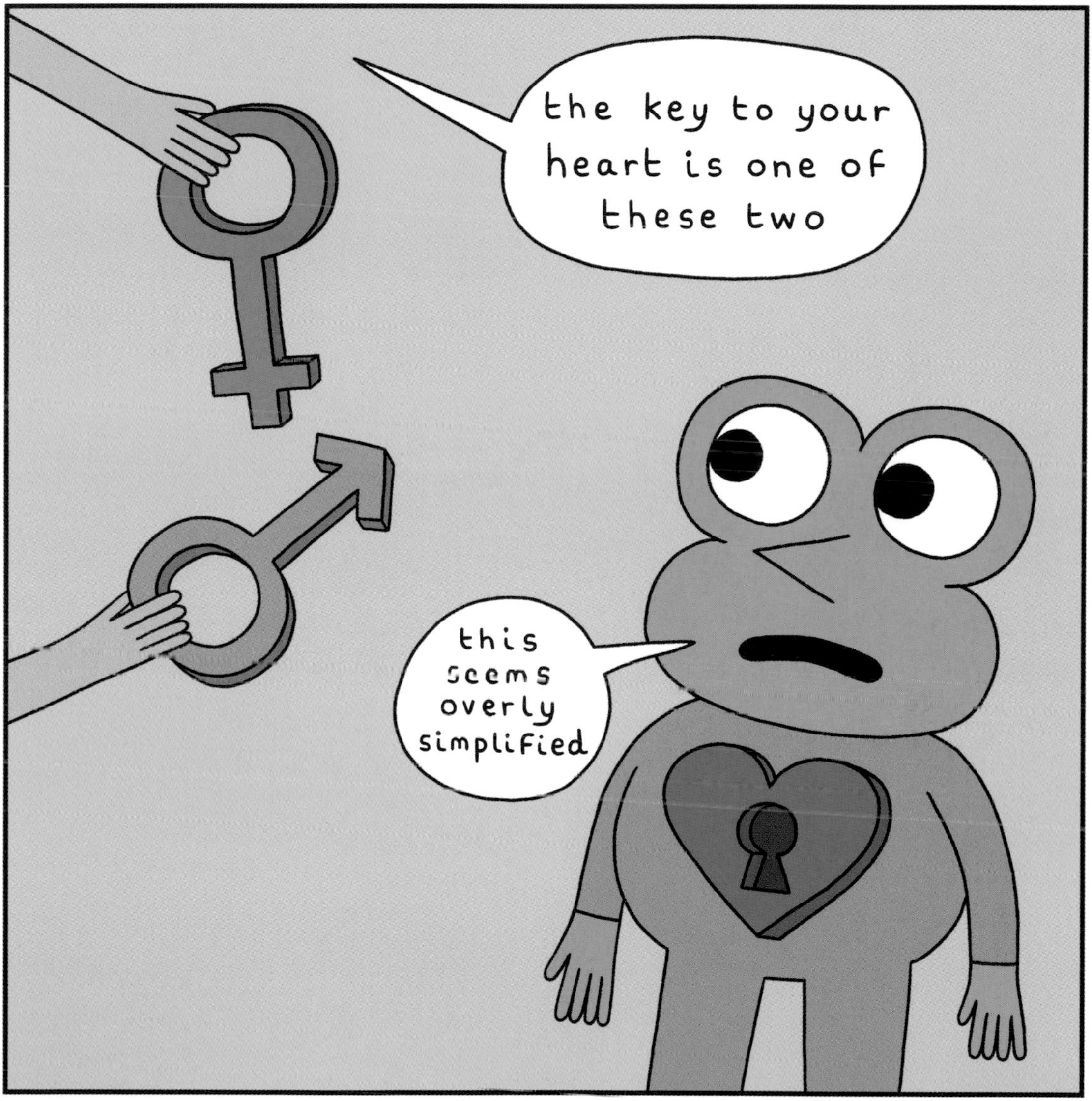

the key to your heart is one of these two
this seems overly simplified

From the moment you are born

you are expected to perform gender in a particular way

even if you would rather express it differently

and be more playful and explorative.

One of these expectations

is that you should only desire people of the "opposite" gender.

Doing anything differently is considered deviating from what is "normal"

and you can be stigmatized for it.

It is weird how fixated
on gender society can be

there's more to me than my gender

when there are so many
other characteristics that
attract us to someone.

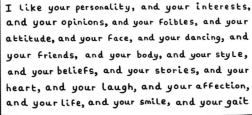

I like your personality, and your interests,
and your opinions, and your foibles, and your
attitude, and your face, and your dancing, and
your friends, and your body, and your style,
and your beliefs, and your stories, and your
heart, and your laugh, and your affection,
and your life, and your smile, and your gait

Everyone has different
things that are important
in a Beloved.

and my gender?

yes it is part of you and I like you

Gender can be part
of that, or not.

If it is, there are many ways to play around
with traditional gender roles.

It can be challenging to
look beyond what we are
told we should feel

and actually understand
what and who we desire

free from outside control
and free from shame.

WHERE CAN I FIND LOVE?

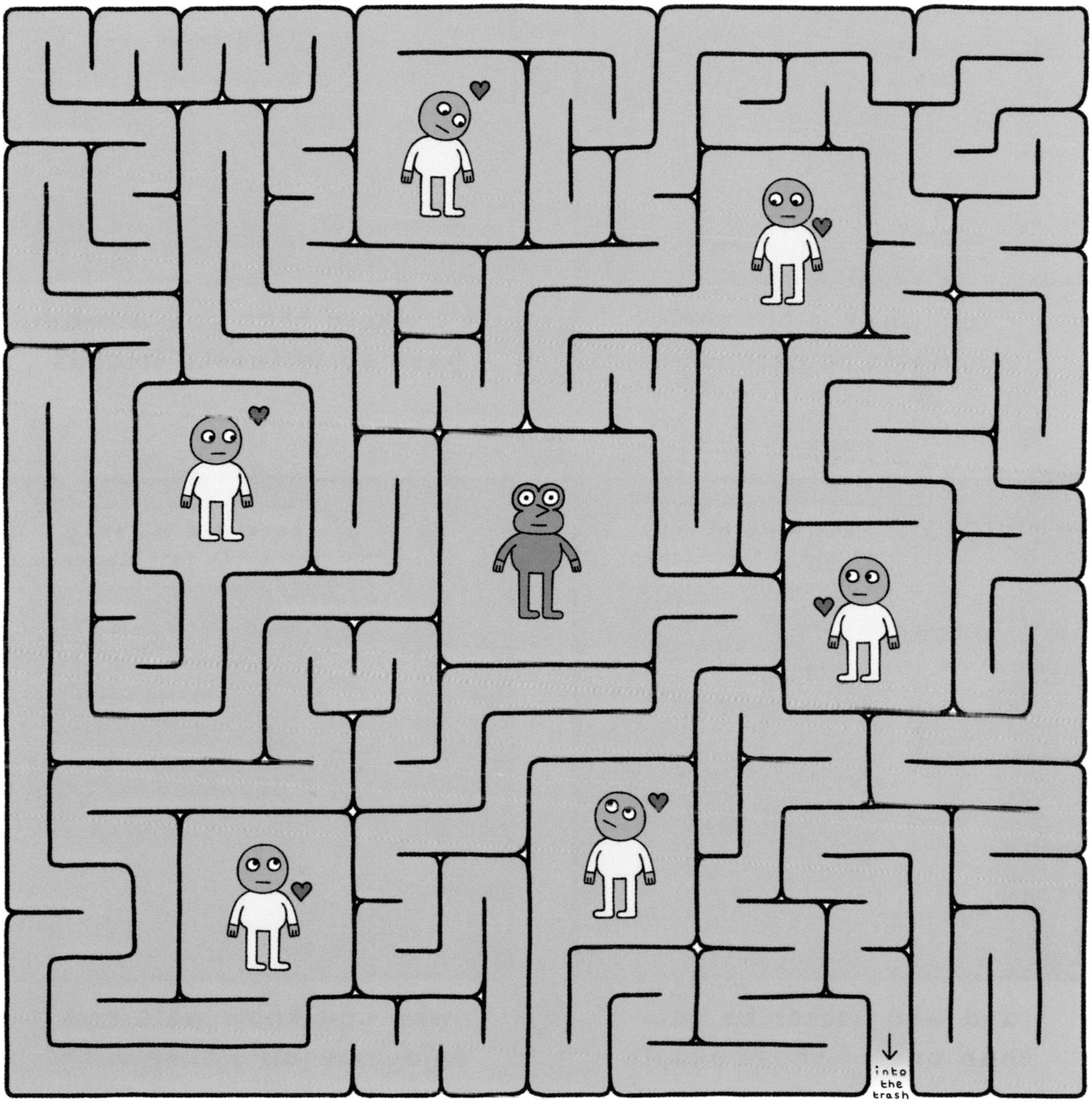
into the trash

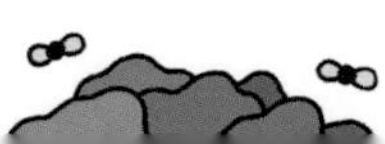

You want a big sexy
romantic relationship.

It's likely that you already
have some lovely friends

and who better to date
than one of those people

who you know well and
enjoy spending time with?

Developing a friendship
into something romantic
can be a beautiful thing

but romantic love
can also be messy

and you may choose not
to risk complicating your
lovely friendships.

In this case, you need to
make new connections.

Going on dates may suit you

because it is a formal, structured way to meet new people.

You may like meeting people at parties

for something more organic and casual.

You may try a new hobby, which can widen your social circle.

Even if you don't find romance, you will be learning new skills

and perhaps, among all these new people, there will be someone you like.

But liking someone doesn't mean you have found love.

That's just the first step.

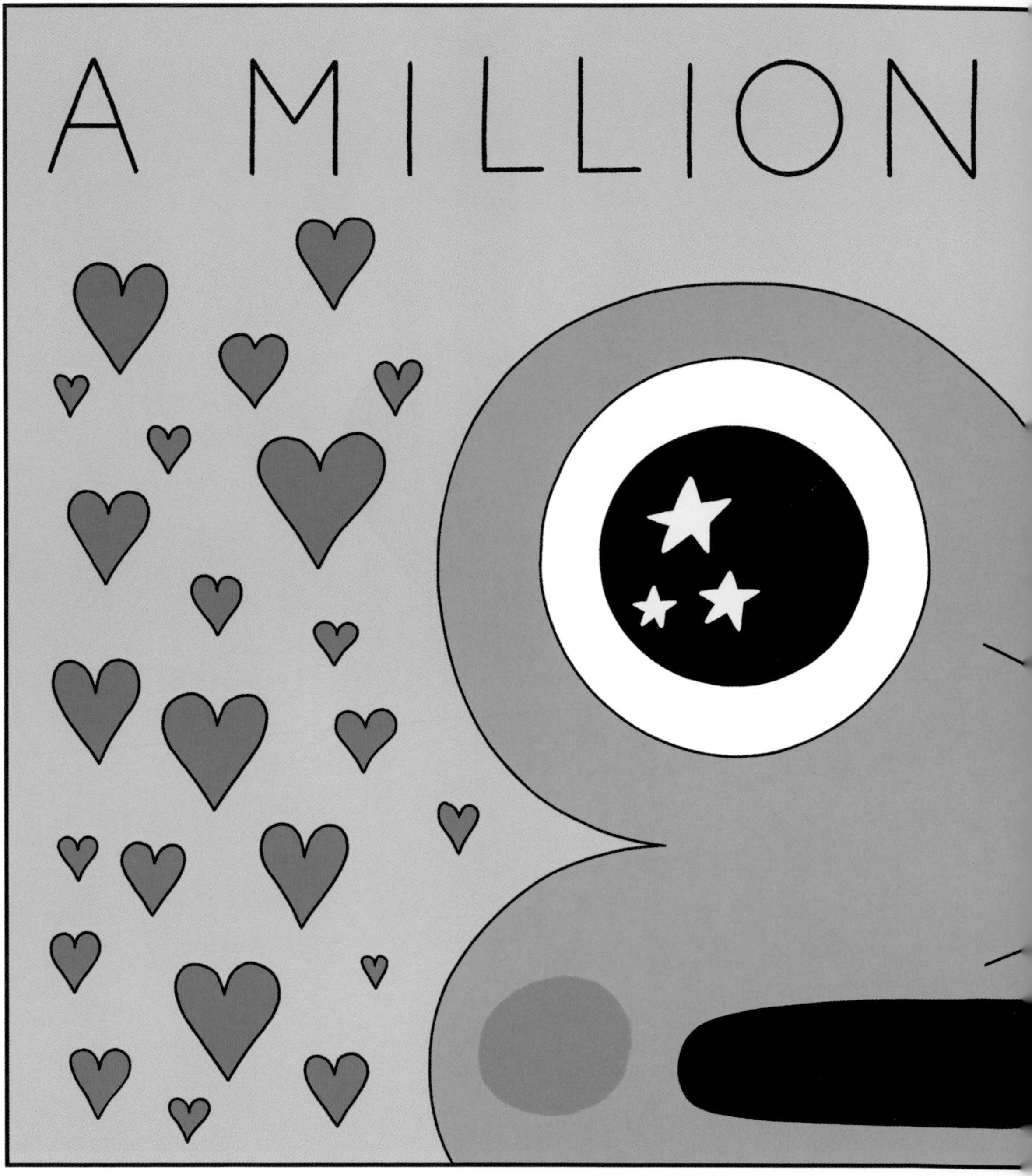
A MILLION

FEELINGS

QUESTIONS ABOUT
FALLING IN LOVE

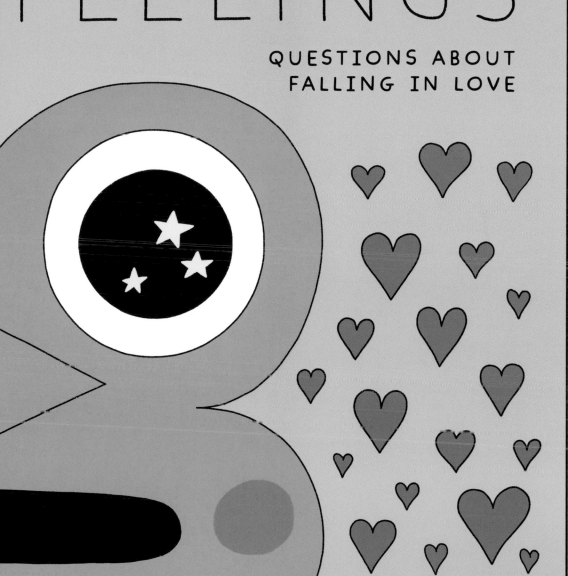

WHY AM I SO AWKWARD AROUND MY CRUSH?

You may feel that you should never have to compromise who you are.

Or you may worry about being overly accommodating.

But being a bit squishy and flexible

can be a good thing.

When you encounter
new people

it helps you to fit together.

The problems come when
you encounter someone

you really, really like.

It is called a "crush"

because it can completely flatten you.

It can make you care so much about being liked

that you may forget who you are

and try to change

in order to be liked.

If you are someone who is weird around your crushes

find someone who likes that about you.

Then you can get weird
and squishy together.

IS IT LOVE OR IS IT LUST?

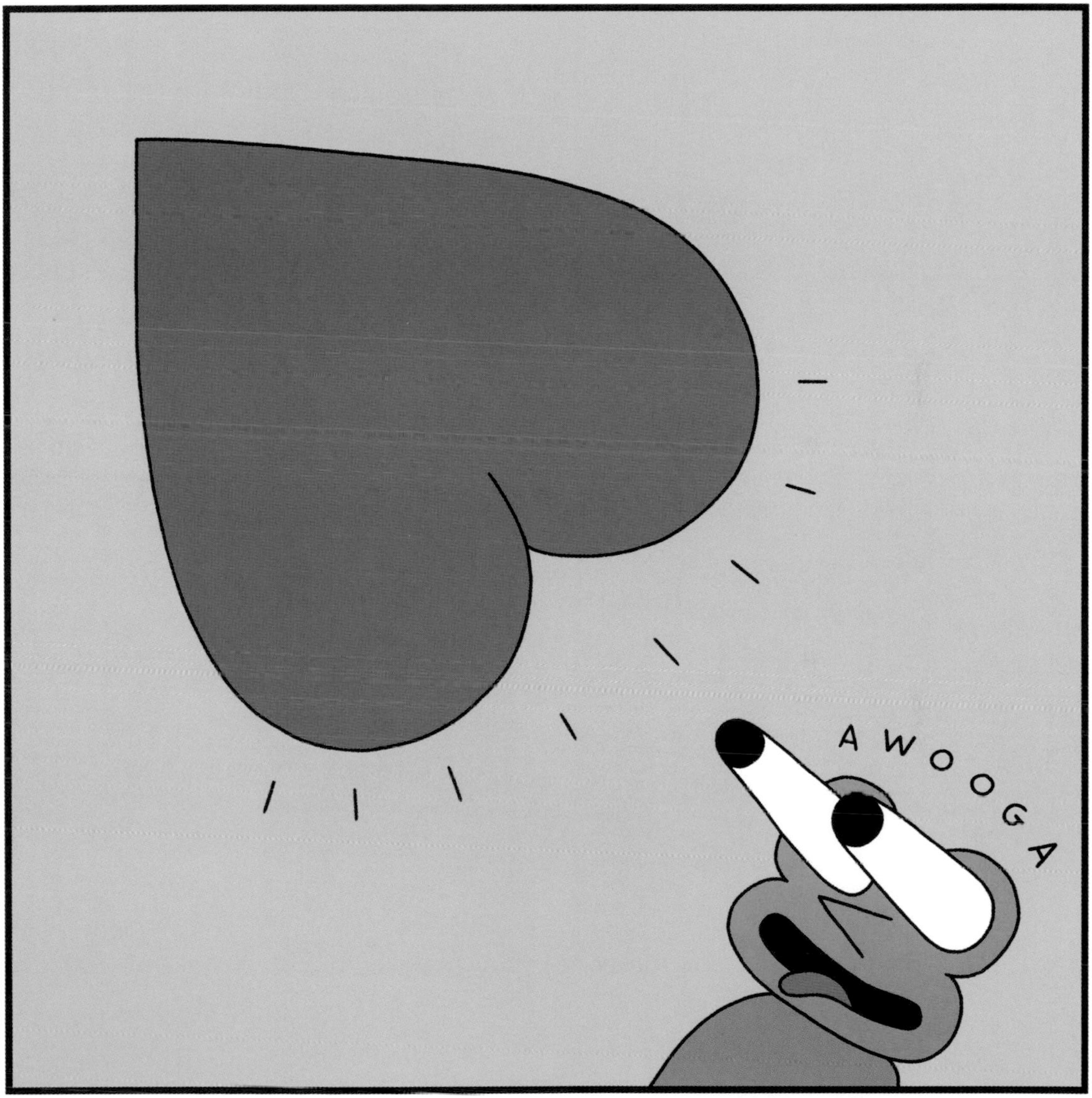
AWOOGA

You can't love someone
you don't know very well

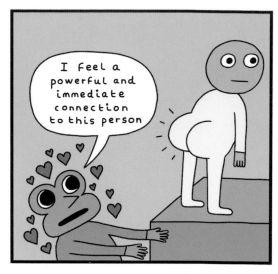

because at first you can
only really see the surface.

You are horny, and
that's okay.

But what are you
actually horny for?

You can be horny for sexiness

horny for support and comfort

horny to know someone
better, and to be known

horny for playfulness and fun.

But just because two
people are attracted

doesn't mean they will
definitely be compatible.

One person may
desire something

and the other person may
desire something else.

Sadly, we can't read minds

so if you want to know what
the other person desires

the closest thing we have to
psychic powers is talking.

Then you can make sure
you are both horny
for the same thing

which was probably what you
were horny for all along.

WHAT IF I LIKE SOMEONE WHO IS OUT OF MY LEAGUE?

You may feel like you've
been put in a box

and that the person you
like is on another level

so you can never be together.

But if you can think
outside of that box

and give yourself a chance
to really look around

you might find that not everyone judges each
other based on the same criteria

and you will see that the hierarchy is just an illusion.

That doesn't guarantee
the person you like
will agree with you.

You might just see things
in different ways.

But if you focus on finding
other people you like

with whom you see eye to eye
on what's truly important

they can make you feel
on top of the world.

WHY DO I ALWAYS FALL FOR BAD BOYS?

Life can be boring.

Sometimes you don't want someone

who just fits in.

You want to shake things up.

Relationships can be a
perfect place for rebellion

a place to find a teammate
who excites you

who challenges you

and supports you as you
break away from how
things were before.

It can be exciting to get close to someone so different

but when you are with a person who always goes their own way

it can feel like you are just along for the ride.

Look at how they
treat other people

and you.

Are they only nice if you go
along with what they want?

You may like how they
push boundaries

but make sure they
respect yours.

HOW DO I ASK SOMEONE OUT?

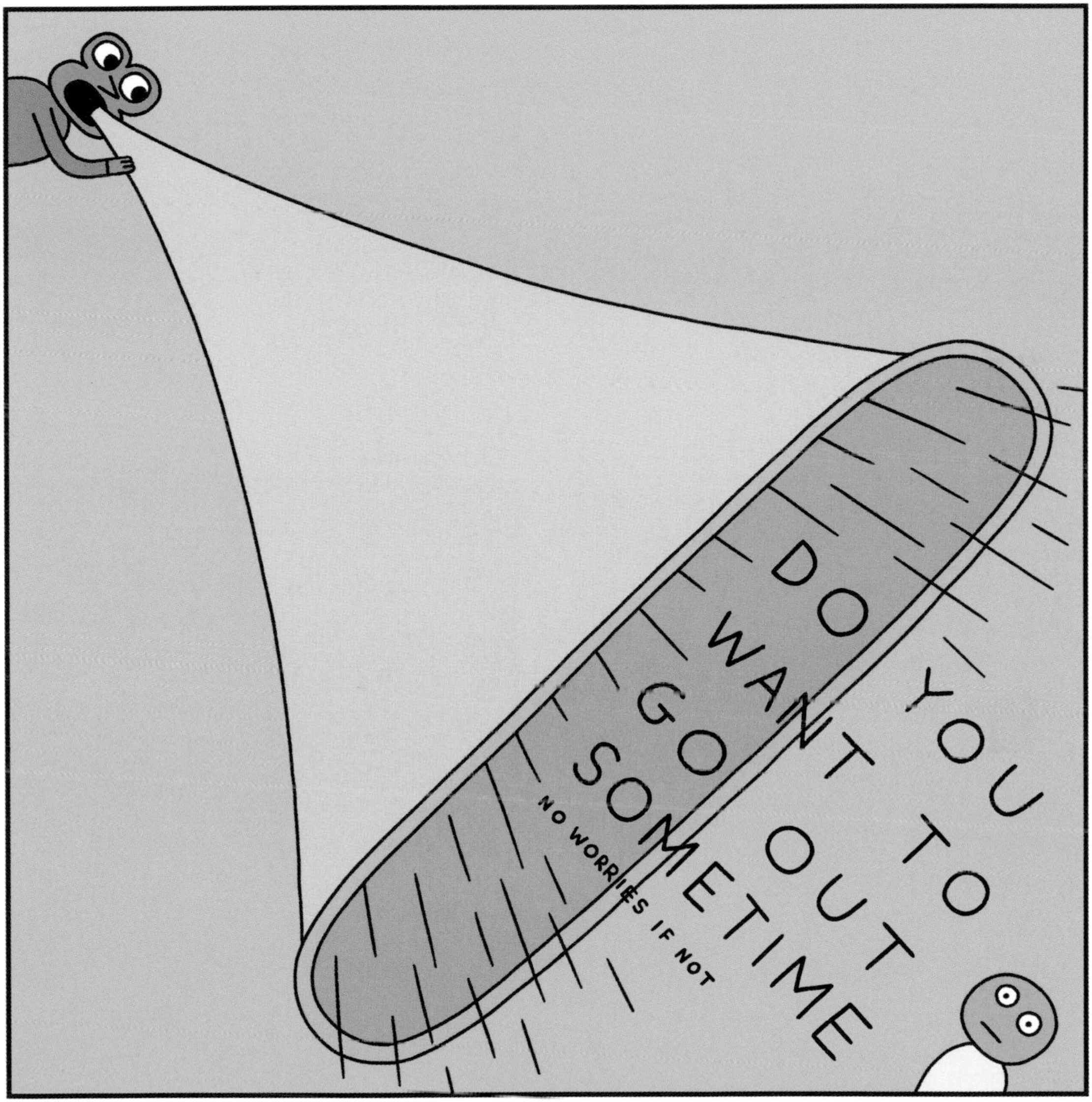

DO YOU WANT TO GO OUT SOMETIME
NO WORRIES IF NOT

It can be scary

to put yourself out there

and make yourself vulnerable

in case you're let down.

Maybe you want to
be approached.

It's nice to feel wanted.

But if you only date
people who approach you

then you only get to date
people who approach you.

This doesn't mean you should ask out just anyone

if you don't know whether that will be okay with them.

Instead, look for someone who's in a similar place to you

and then be direct about
what you're looking for.

Love is complicated
enough as it is.

Have a few friends
on standby in case
you are let down

and be clear and open
about what you want

so you can get a clear reply.

WHAT IF THEY SAY NO?

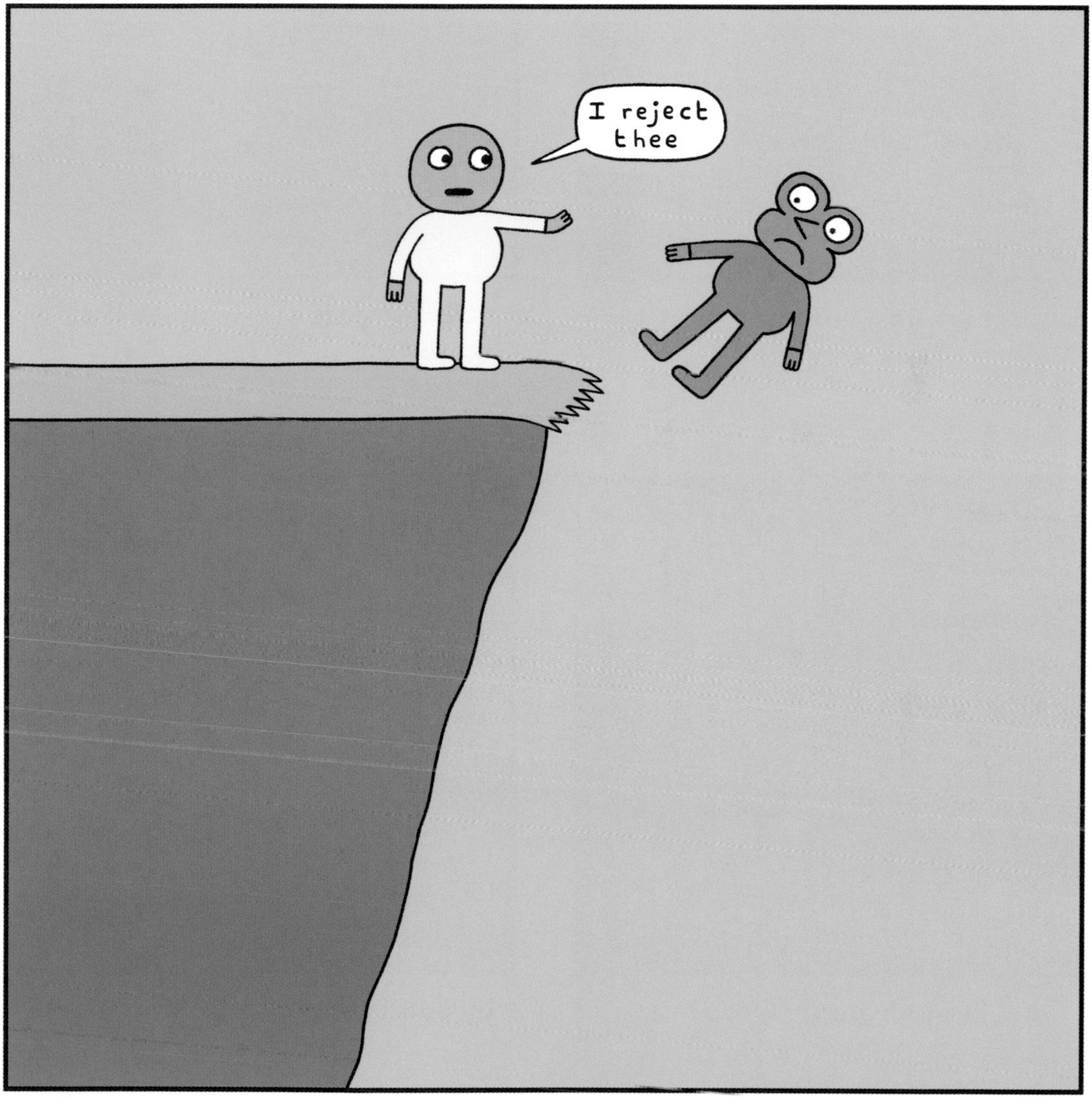
I reject thee

When you have feelings
for someone

they can seem powerful

as though your well-being

is completely in their hands.

From another perspective

your Beloved is the one put in a tricky position

where not accepting your affection

can feel like a brutal act.

Much of the worst
pain of rejection

is the pain we cause
ourselves afterward

and it is important not
to take this out on

the person who has
set a boundary.

Remember you are the one
with power over your feelings.

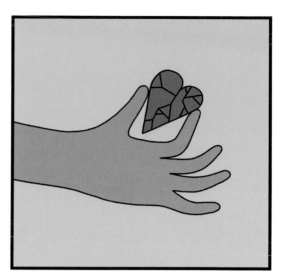

There will be times
when you feel hurt

but these are the times it is most important

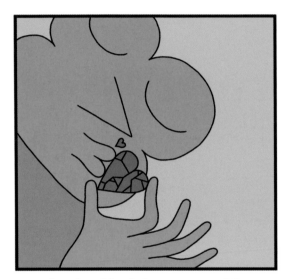

to be kind to yourself.

WHAT IF THEY GIVE ME MIXED SIGNALS?

You are a feelings detective

being sneaky and investigative

collecting clues

and trying to identify how your Beloved feels about you.

All you want is for the mystery to be solved—even
if the conclusion isn't what you hoped.

If your Beloved reveals that
they feel the same way

your detective work is done.

Then you can be open and
honest about your feelings.

But if they are still being
mysterious and unclear

if they say they like
you but don't show it

or they act differently
in different situations

then the mystery is not
solved after all.

You deserve clarity
and openness

and if they can't
give that to you

the new question is:
Am I enjoying this?

And this is a mystery you
can solve for yourself.

WHAT IF THEY AREN'T WHO I THOUGHT?

When you are drawing, it is important to look at your subject properly.

You may have an idea of what it should look like

and end up missing all the interesting, surprising details

that make the subject what it is.

Similarly, when you are
ready to love someone

you may have a type
of person in mind

and you begin to see
what you want to see

in your potential Beloved.

You can get quite deep
into a relationship

while still not really knowing
who your partner is.

Down the line

you have
only painted
my snout

it can lead to disappointment
and confusion

when your partner isn't who you thought.

They may feel unappreciated

and you may miss signs your Beloved isn't right for you.

So make sure you
look properly.

CAN I LOVE MORE THAN ONE PERSON?

Romantic comedies

explore love's challenges
and dilemmas.

A love triangle is a classic
rom-com dilemma.

Love between more than two
people is seen as a problem

because in the end, only
one Beloved can be chosen.

When characters love
more than one person

it is usually in secretive,
deceitful ways

where one person comes at
the expense of the other.

This dilemma does not exist with other types of relationships.

When we have a new friend or family member

our love for them is added to the pile.

Loving many people at once is not an alien concept.

Rom-coms often find creative ways to make one person in the love triangle an obvious choice.

But rarely do they explore ways of resolving it

where everyone is aware and having a lovely time

and it isn't a dilemma at all.

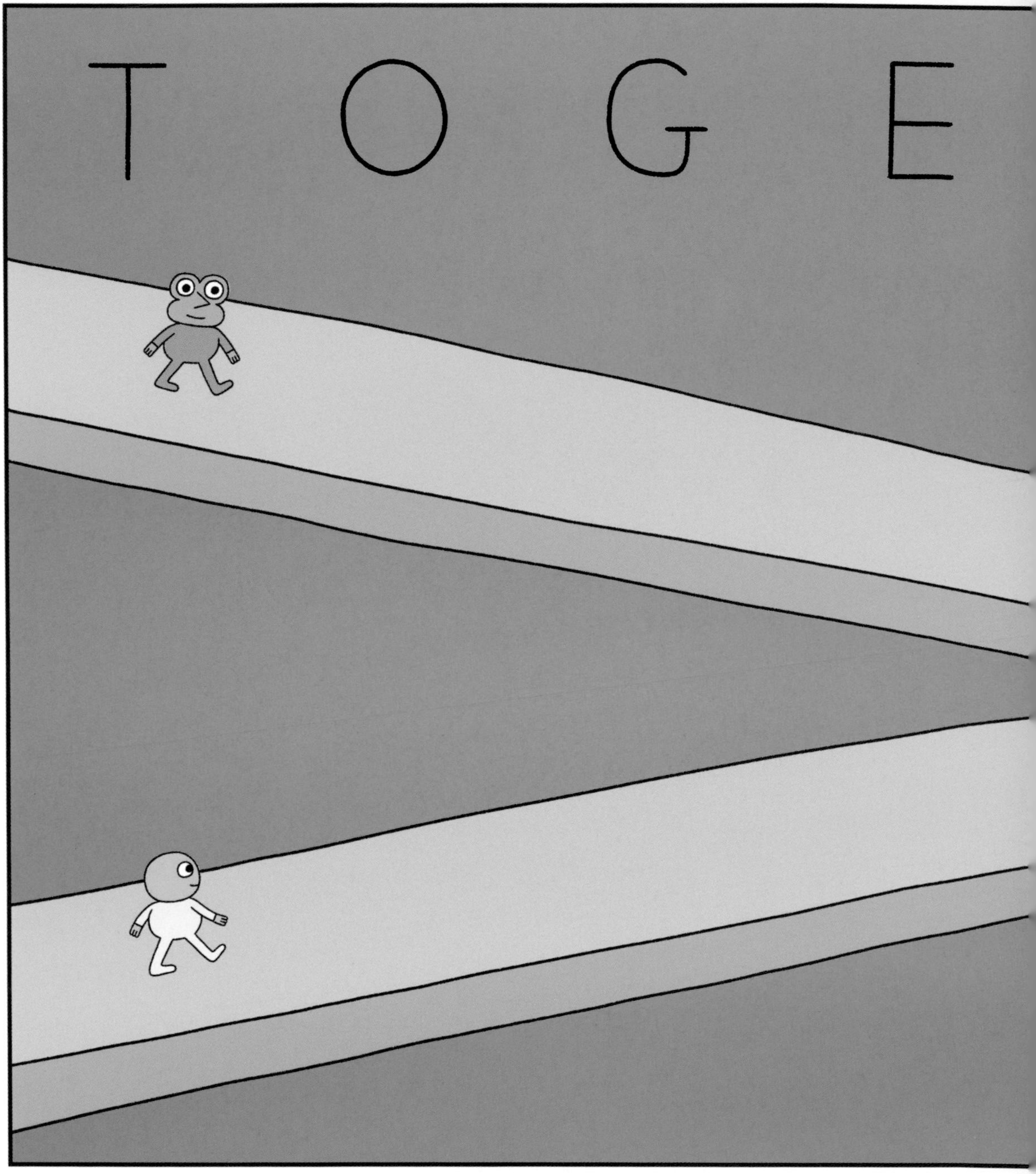
T O G E

THER

QUESTIONS ABOUT BEING
IN A RELATIONSHIP

WHAT SHOULD OUR RELATIONSHIP LOOK LIKE?

The relationships you embark on can take many forms.

If it is a friendship, your relationship can be pretty much any shape or size

and you can build it in whatever way works best for you both.

But of all the types
of relationship

there is one we consider
the ultimate

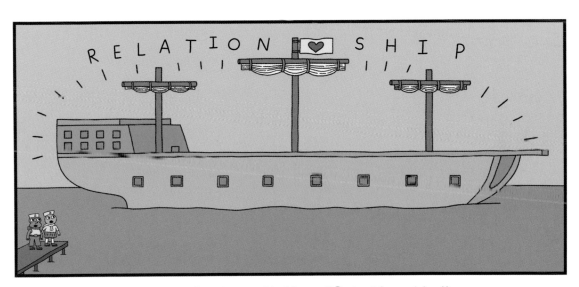

so we simply call it a "Relationship."

It comes with many rules
and expectations

which can be very daunting

and when your
Relationship isn't a shape
you have designed

you may end up maintaining
elements you never wanted.

It's sad that we often think of Relationships and friendships as entirely separate things

when such a big Relationship will feel hollow if you aren't friends first and foremost.

If you think of a Relationship as a big friendship, it will be less daunting.

You will feel more able to build a connection that suits you

and it can be just as
huge and majestic.

HOW CAN I BE ROMANTIC?

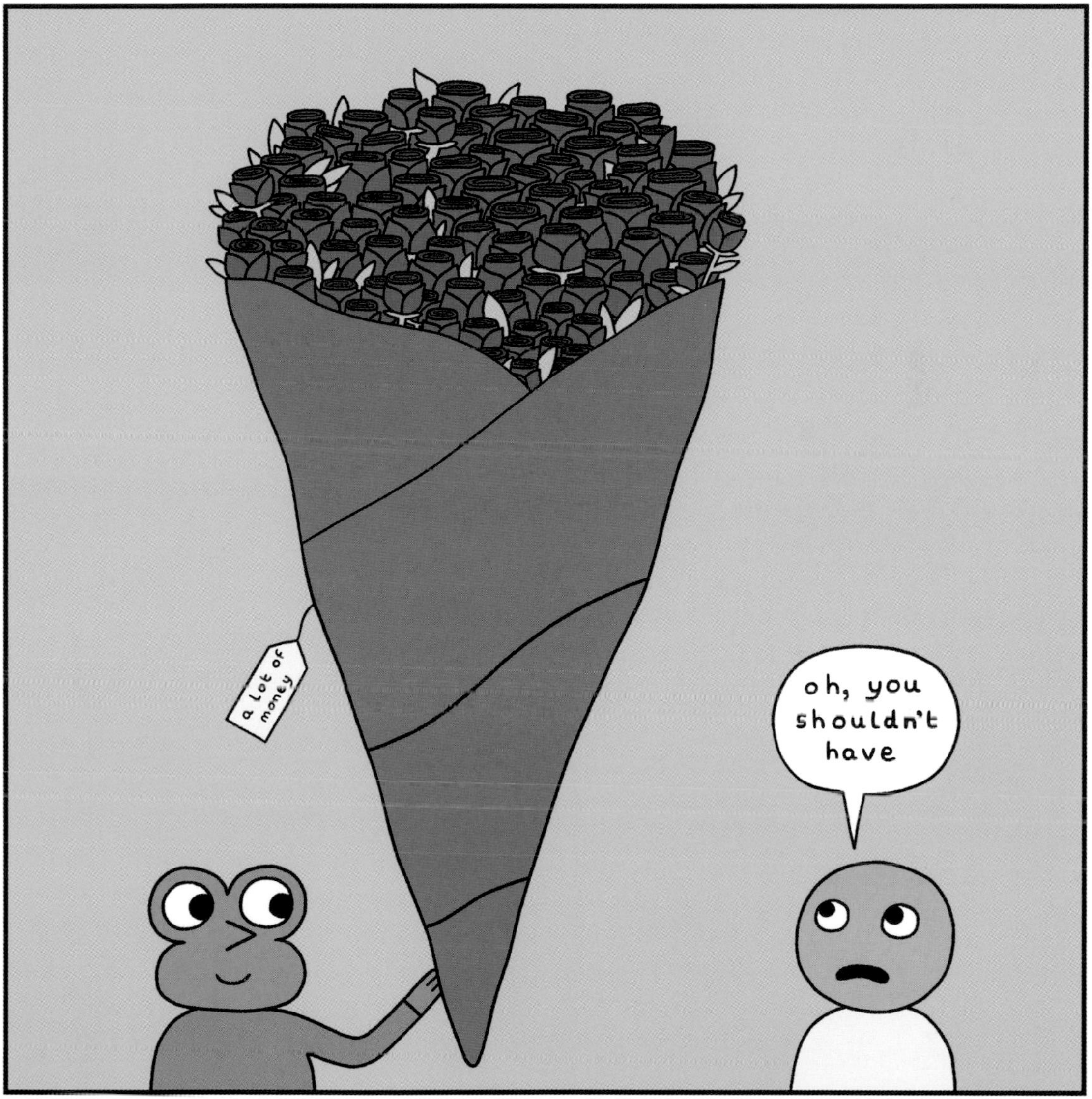
a lot of money
oh, you shouldn't have

When you are in love,
you have a lot of intense
feelings to express.

You want to throw a
birthday party for them
each night in their dreams

bathe them in your
tears until their
fingertips go wrinkly

spend two hundred years
as a hermit contemplating
their earlobe.

Romantic gestures are supposed to be the ways we express and celebrate our unique feelings of love.

But, ironically, these gestures tend to be the ways

our relationships are most similar to everyone else's.

When you struggle to express
your ineffable emotions

it can be fun to
recreate what we see
in books and movies

but sometimes we do
"romantic" things

because we think it's what
we are supposed to do.

But a safe, intimate relationship

is surely the perfect place

to go beyond social conventions

and build a personal language of affection.

What is more romantic
than that?

HOW DO I KNOW HOW FAST OR SLOW TO TAKE THINGS?

You are on the path of love, crossing
markers of progress along the way.

These markers may feel like
a test of your relationship

as though you should be
as committed to the path
as you are to each other.

You may feel pressure to
go as fast as possible

as though you have
somewhere to get to

rather than enjoying the journey and
making a path of your own.

The best paths are made
by seeking out things
you are excited to do

and excited to do together.

You may come across terrain
you aren't sure about

and it's important you
take the time to reflect.

One person may be more
prepared for the next step

but it is important not to
drag the other along.

It may be that the path
simply needs to take
another direction

or it may be that your
paths start to diverge

and you simply aren't
compatible travel companions.

IS IT OKAY IF WE ARGUE A LOT?

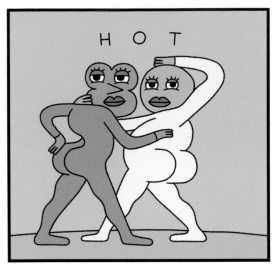

When two hotties
are together

sometimes things get heated.

An important part of
any relationship

is being able to talk through
these problems together.

We might justify drama by thinking it shows we care

but speaking angrily may prevent you from being properly heard

or prevent your Beloved from speaking openly in return

which means you aren't communicating well.

Relationships should be
mostly nice times.

If you are constantly
putting out fires

and you are only happy when
things are briefly calm

then your relationship won't
be a nice place to be.

If you are able to
communicate calmly

and try to solve your
problems together

then your arguments
will feel constructive
rather than destructive

so you can focus less
on putting out fires

and focus more on
being hotties.

WHY DO PEOPLE ABANDON THEIR FRIENDS WHEN THEY FIND LOVE?

In many stories, friends
are just sidekicks.

No matter how deep
the friendship

as soon as the love
interest arrives

the friend is sidelined.

Sometimes friendships
change, or end.

This can be difficult
to deal with when you
are "just" the friend

especially because you
may feel that such
intense feelings

are not valid when it
comes to friendships.

We often use phrases like
"more than friends"

as though friendship is lesser

despite good friendships
being just as likely

to be intense, enjoyable,
and long-lasting.

Hopefully, you and your friend are able to talk through it.

New love doesn't have to come at the expense of old love.

Life is always more than one story

and you can be part of
many adventures.

HOW DO I MAKE THINGS SEXY?

Sexiness isn't all about
tips, tricks, and techniques

or feats of incredible
physical prowess.

If you have too many
expectations of how
sexiness should go

then you won't be paying
attention to what your
partner actually wants.

We often neglect sensuality

which is enjoying your
feelings and sensations
in the moment

and being connected
to your body and the
world around you.

If you learn to notice
nice feelings

savor pleasure

relax, and feel held

then you'll be more
in tune with yourself
and your partner

and enjoy all stages
of intimacy.

By going slowly, you can communicate with your bodies

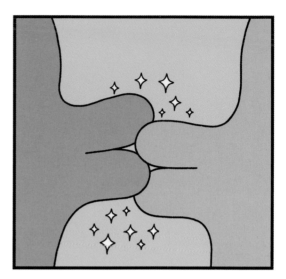

and be more tuned in to what your partner does and doesn't like.

I don't know what I am doing

If you aren't fully sure

there is a simple technique you can do with your tongue and lips:

149

TALK

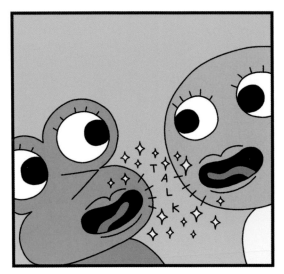

talk through it.

IS JEALOUSY GOOD OR BAD?

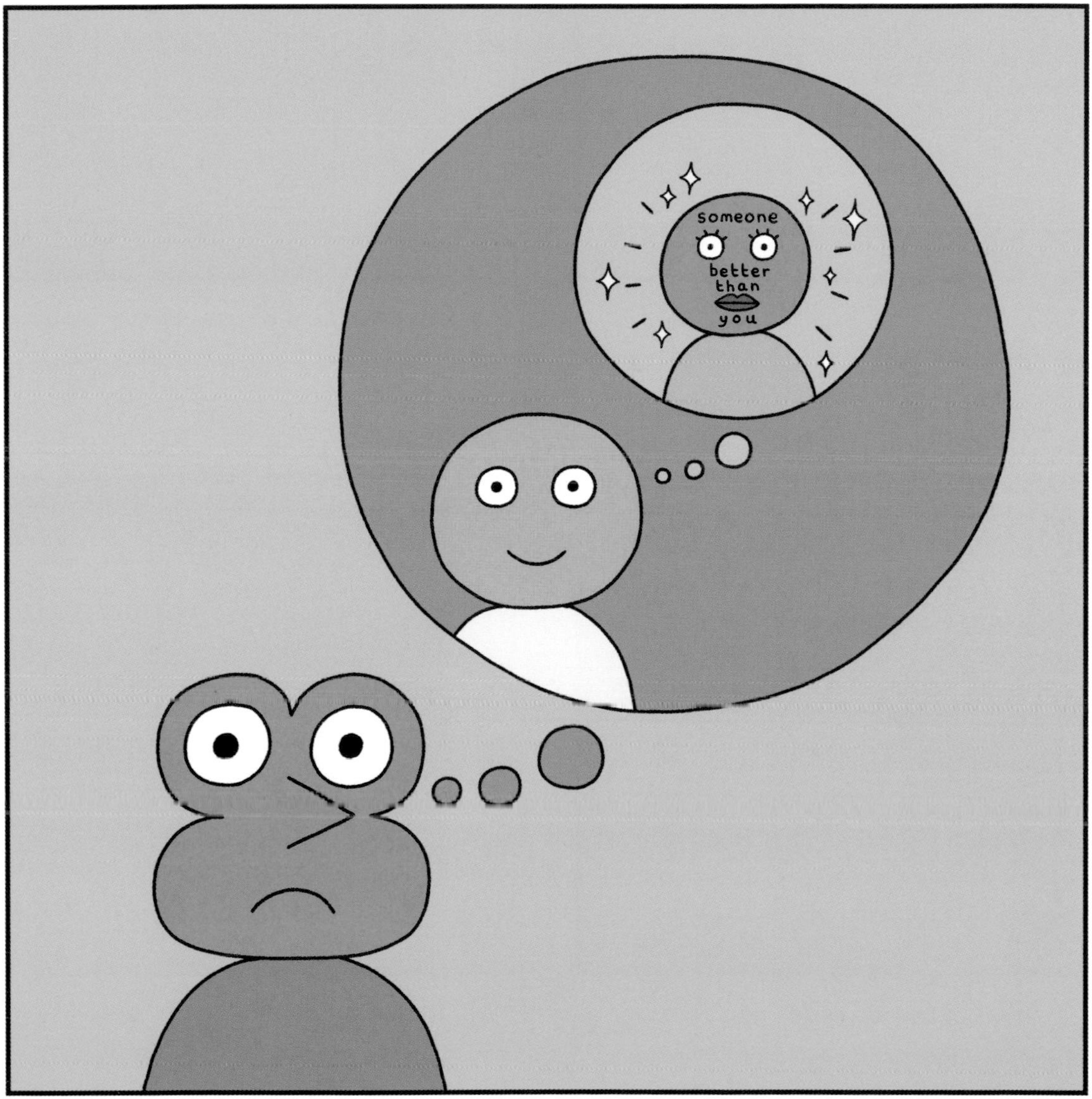
someone
better
than
you

You may think that
jealousy is a good thing

because it shows that you
care about your Beloved.

But sometimes you may
focus more on defending
your relationship

than making it a
nice place to be.

You can't be everything
to each other

and no matter how high you
build the walls, jealousy
will always show up.

The outside world won't feel so threatening if you
make a relationship you feel confident in.

Feelings of jealousy aren't bad if you are able to communicate well.

They can help you work out the source of your insecurities

so you can work together

to maintain a strong, secure relationship.

Then you can feel good
about each other's lives
outside your relationship.

This is sort of the opposite of
jealousy, called "compersion."

Your separate lives do not
have to come at the expense
of your life together.

In fact, your life inside
your relationship will
be made even better

when it is more open
to the outside.

CAN A LONG-DISTANCE RELATIONSHIP WORK?

You probably like to spend a lot of time with your Beloved

and be physically close.

This is difficult when you are far away.

Technology makes it
easier to connect

and support each
other from afar

and for some people
this is great!

We all have different
needs for intimacy.

But it can be difficult to be dependent on someone

when the situation prevents you from supporting each other.

In the short term, this can be bearable

but sometimes we can hang on

longing for a rose-tinted past

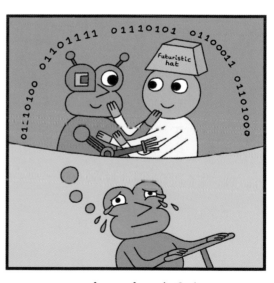

or an imagined future

rather than being
happy right now.

WHEN IS THE RIGHT TIME TO FIRST SAY "I LOVE YOU"?

When you say "I love you" for the first time

it is not just an expression of your feelings.

You also expect a reply from your Beloved

to confirm you are in a committed, secure relationship.

But this shouldn't be
a test of whether your
Beloved loves you back.

They likely have lots of
wonderful feelings for you

but may need more time
to explore and understand
these feelings

before committing to
saying "I love you."

Of course it's no fun to be
with someone who doesn't
make you feel loved

but you can both show
affection in many
different ways.

There are so many things
you can do for each other

and so many things to say
before "I love you."

The right time to say
these words is when you
know how your Beloved
expresses their love

and your feelings are
already clear in other ways

so you can be fairly sure
they are ready to give the
response you hope for.

Then it isn't a test of
whether they love you or not

it is a confirmation of
what you already know.

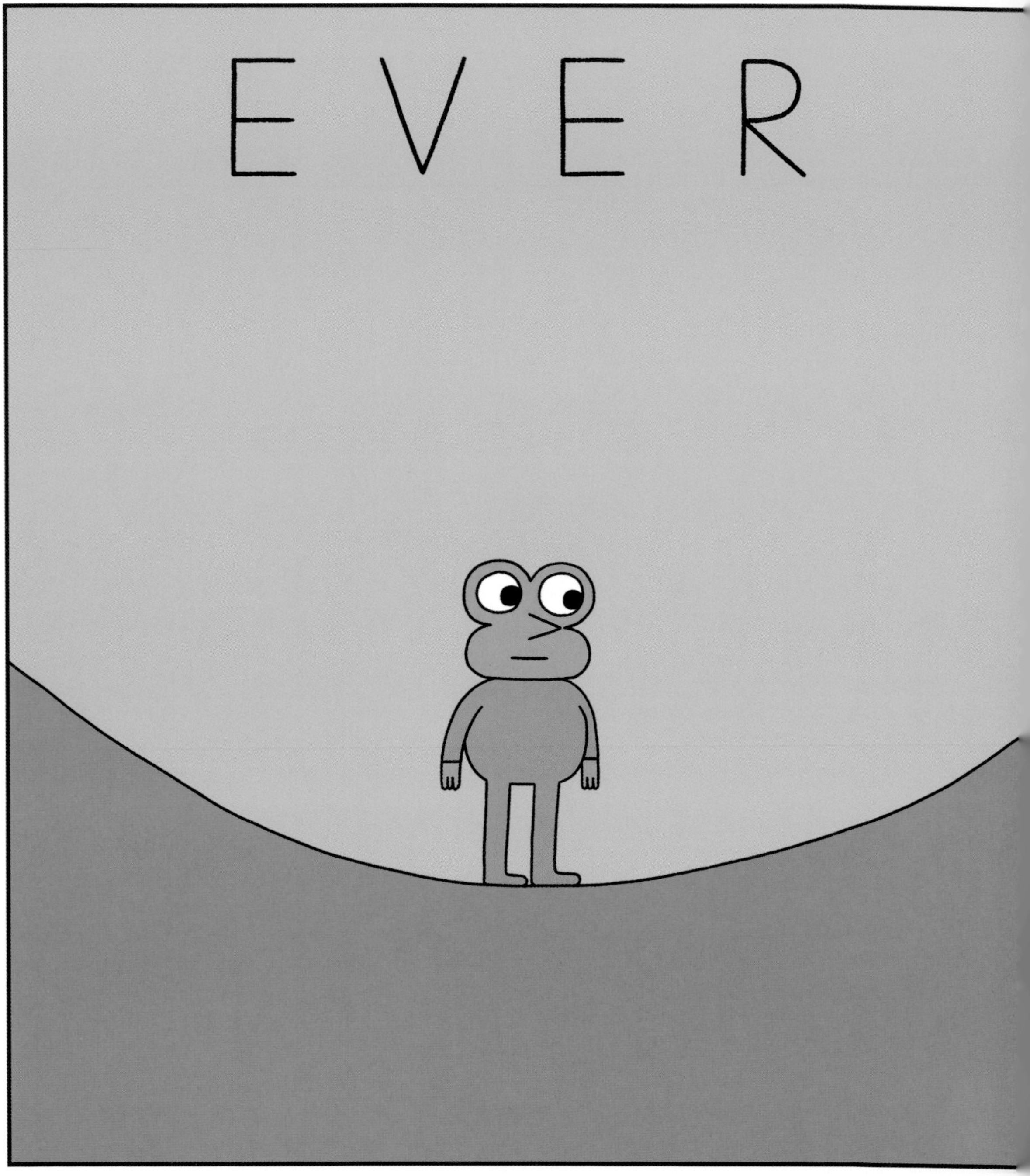
EVER

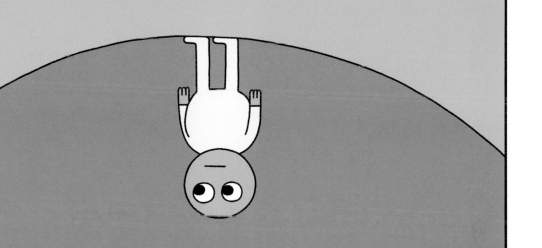

AFTER

QUESTIONS ABOUT
WHAT COMES NEXT

WILL I EVER FIND "THE ONE"?

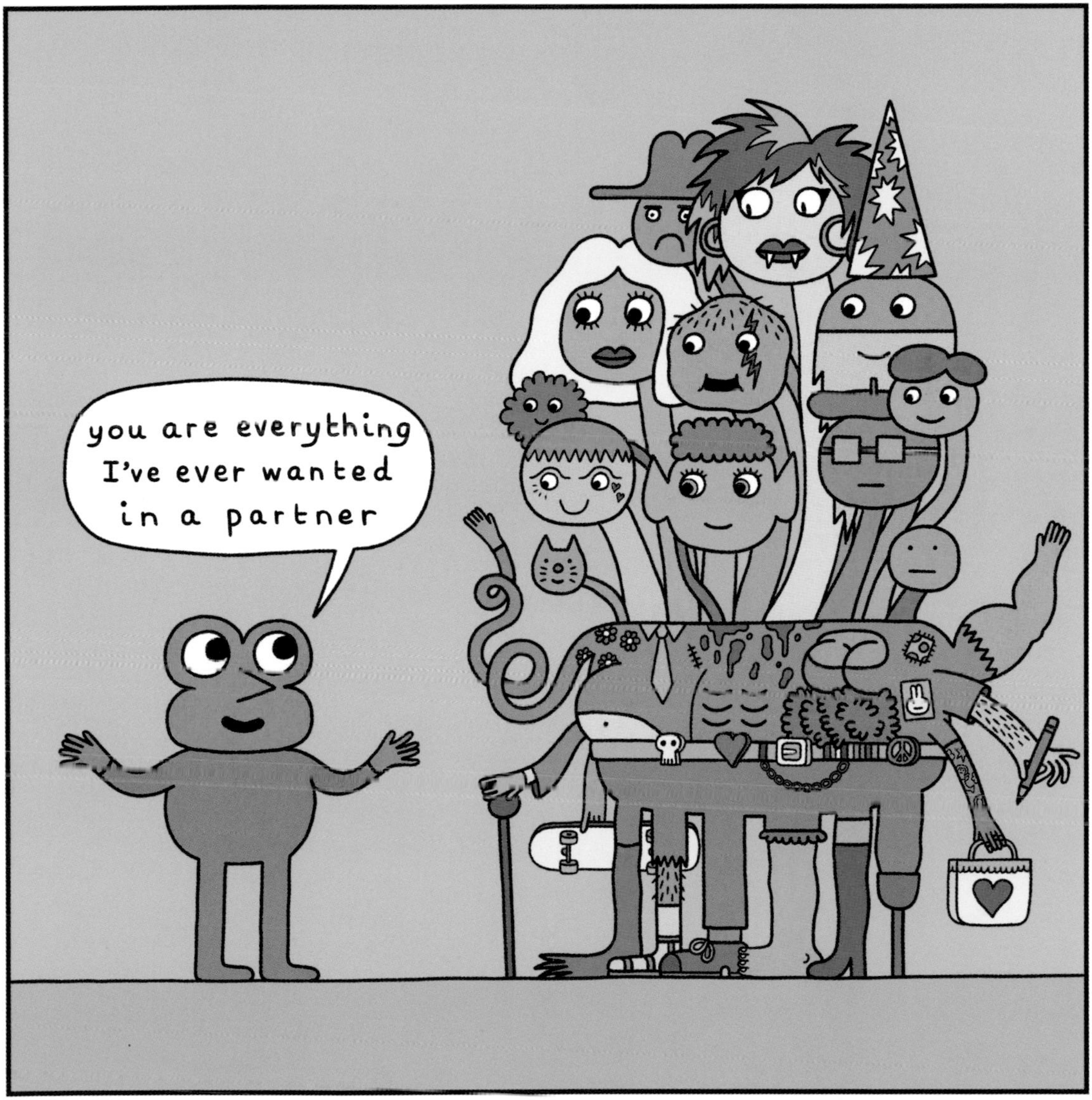
you are everything I've ever wanted in a partner

You know who you are.

You have an idea of who your perfect partner would be.

You feel sure that once you find the one who's a perfect fit

love will flourish easily.

This way of seeing love
assumes it won't change you

and that you will be perfectly
compatible from the start.

So when love requires
work and compromise

you start to think it's
not the right fit.

You don't have to be
compatible right away.

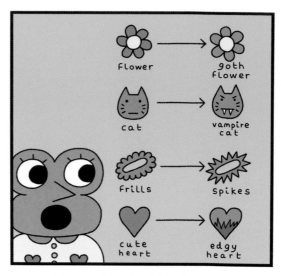

You will both change
and grow as your
connection deepens.

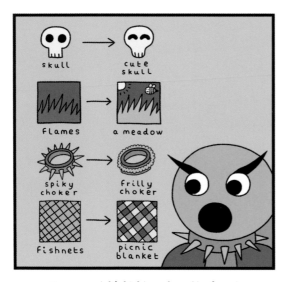

Compatibility isn't just
something you find

it is something you achieve.

But if you could adapt
for this one person

does that mean you
could have made it work
with someone else?

Yes! But not just anyone.

You have found someone
you enjoy changing with

which means it is a
perfect match.

CAN WE "LIVE HAPPILY EVER AFTER"?

Love stories often go
the same way:

there is an obstacle
between the lovers

and they overcome
the obstacle.

The End.

Our idea of romantic
love is usually something
committed and long-lasting

but love stories often
end before we actually
see that develop.

We focus so much on
falling in love

that sometimes it is hard
to know what to do once
we have fallen in.

Your aim may be to
stay together forever

but this aim makes us
more likely to remain
in bad relationships

or, after a while, get complacent.

A successful relationship is
not one without obstacles

it is one where you deal
with obstacles well

and enjoy the times of peace.

Happiness is not a
resting state

it is something you have
to work on together.

CAN I BREAK UP WITH SOMEONE WITHOUT HURTING THEM?

If you are unhappy in your relationship

you may hope things can easily drift apart.

This is unlikely with a big connection.

It will probably be more complicated and painful.

But wanting to abandon the relationship

doesn't necessarily mean you don't care about your partner anymore.

The kindest thing to
do in this situation is
to provide clarity.

This doesn't mean being
cruel and callous.

It means allowing them to
understand what is happening

so they aren't hanging on.

That way, they can
prepare for separation

and can fully feel
how they feel.

Breaking up is tough,
and requires courage.

One of the most difficult
parts of breaking up

is no longer being the ones to
help each other through it.

I GOT DUMPED. WHAT NOW?

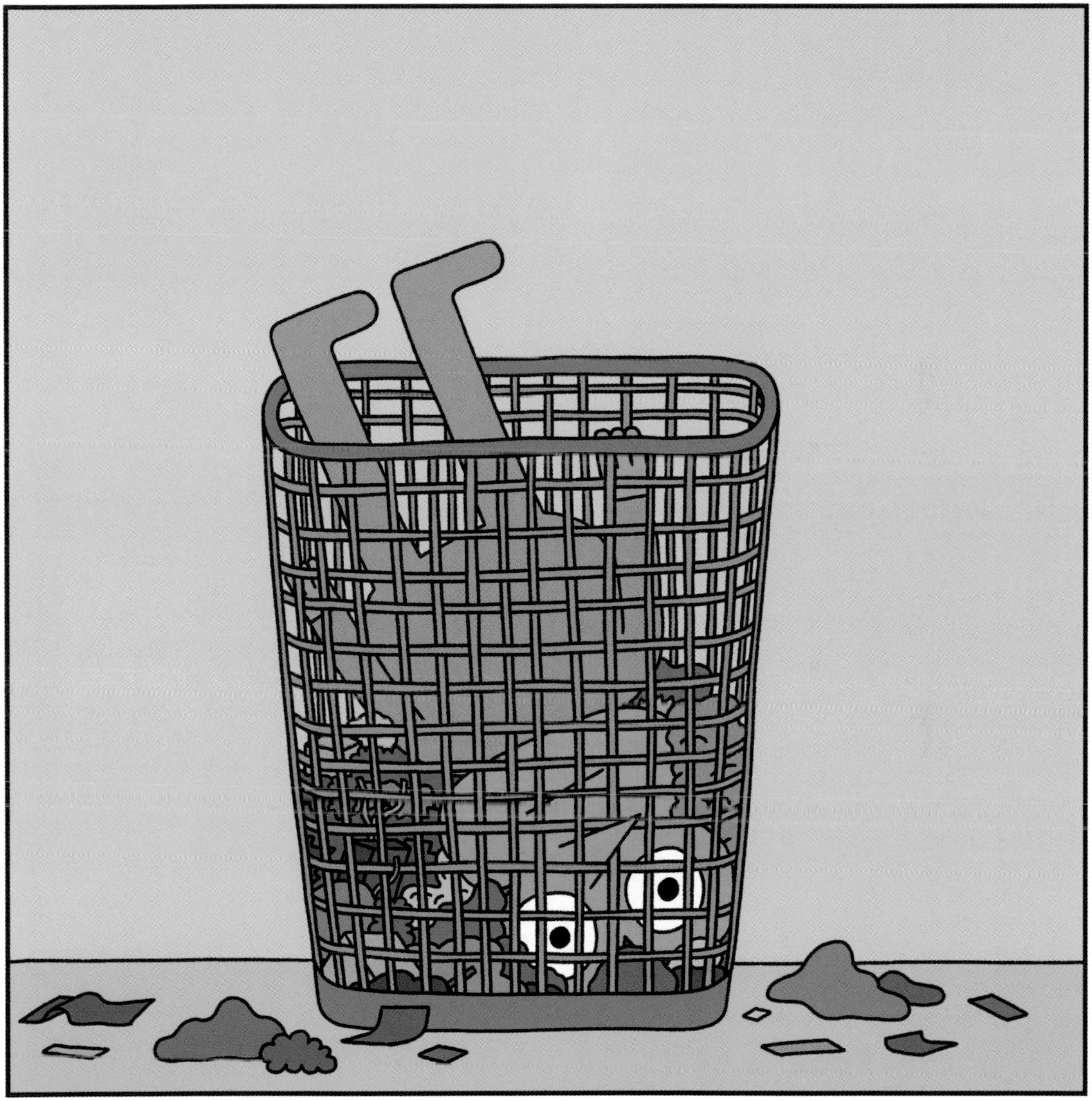

You deserve love and
you deserve happiness.

You aren't feeling those
things right now.

You may be eager not
to feel bad anymore

but you can't rush things.

You won't feel this
way forever.

Just get through it
one day at a time.

Be kind and patient
with yourself.

It is horrible when a
relationship you care about

ends sooner than you hoped.

CAN I BE FRIENDS WITH MY EX?

If you don't work
well together

and the relationship you've
made is a bit of a mess

it might mean that trying a
different sort of relationship

will go just as badly.

Maybe you did work
well together

but if the ingredients
of your relationship
are already cooked

it might be difficult

to transform it into
a new thing.

If you want to remain
friends, you need
to start fresh

and leave things
be for a while.

Spend some time separately.

Meet some new people.

Maybe you'll decide you don't need that friendship
when you discover so many new connections.

Or maybe you'll come
back together

with some fresh ingredients

ready to make a delicious
new friendship.

HOW DO I MOVE ON?

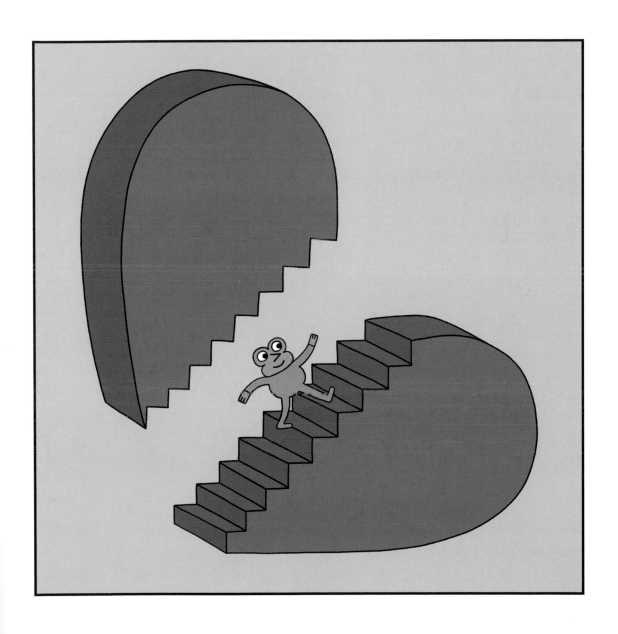

Even if you wanted
things to end

the aftermath can be
painful and challenging.

Before you rush into
anything new

you first have to
process stuff.

You may want to simply
get rid of these feelings

and put the whole
thing behind you

but feelings we try
to bury away

tend to grow into
something more.

You need to confront
the painful bits

wallow in your feelings

and the more friends
and hobbies you have

the more easily you will
erode away the sharp edges.

Your old loves will
always be with you

so if you make them
smooth and manageable

they can become part of you

and you can carry them

into whatever you do next.

WILL I EVER LOVE AGAIN?

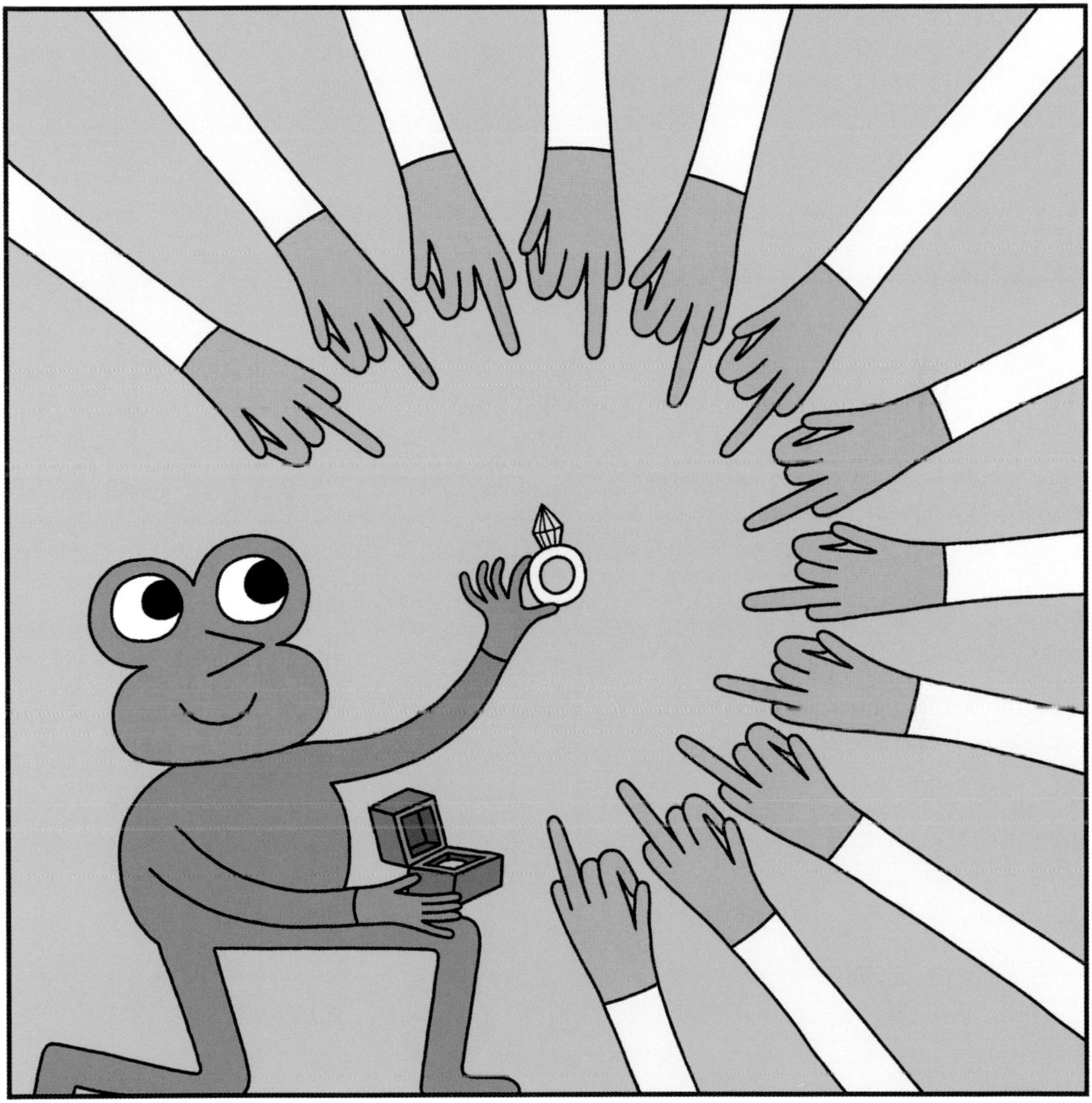

Here you are, again.

Floating through
the void, again.

You loved someone, and it
can be difficult to imagine

replicating that with
someone else.

You will be able to have feelings for new people, in time.

But you will not be able to replicate that previous love

because every person is different and every relationship is unique.

Rather than replicating
your Beloved

think about what you
need in this moment.

You may not need that
exact role filled

to have your needs fulfilled.

You are always changing.

You are not the same person as when you fell in love previously.

The kind of person you need in your life right now

is probably something brand-
new, exciting, and different.

OUTROD

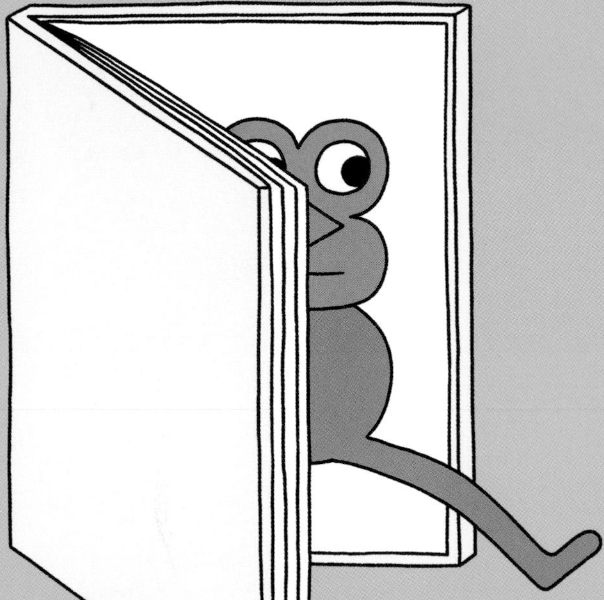

UCTION

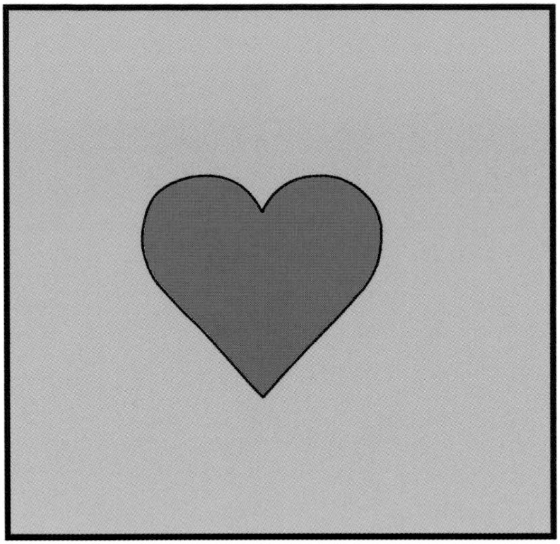

In many ways, this is a good symbol for love.

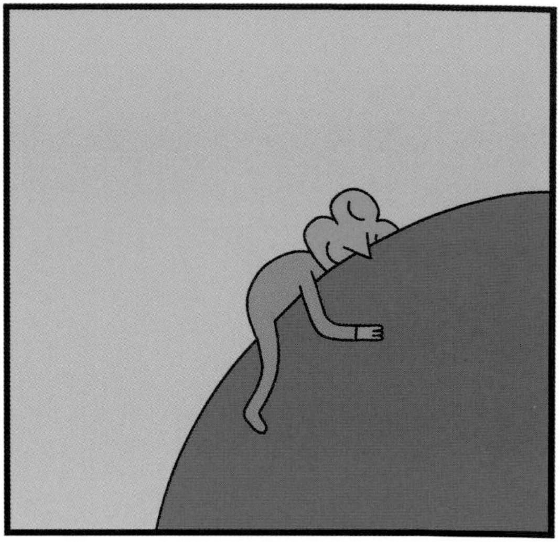

Love can be smooth and comforting

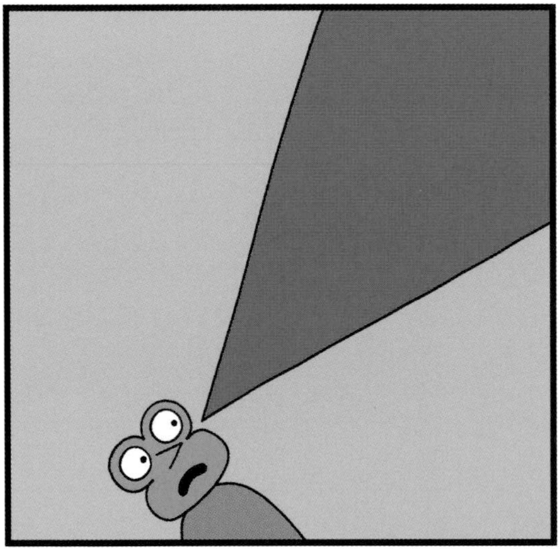

but it can also be sharp and painful

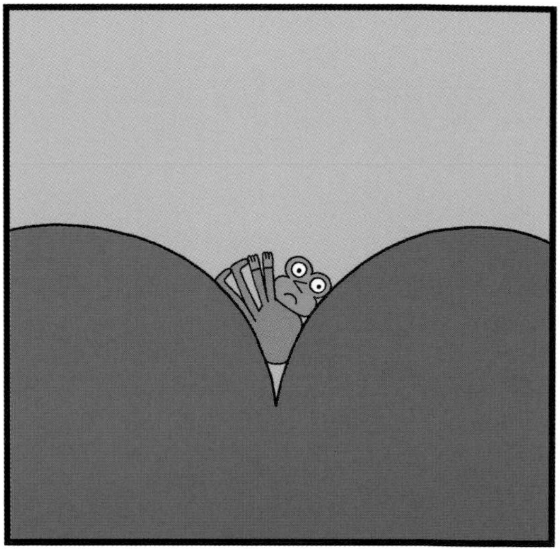

with places where you can feel stuck.

All this book can do
is talk about love in
an abstract way

and even if you read a
lot about love in theory

when you go out into
the real world

you'll find it is incredibly
complicated and messy.

You will need to make your own mistakes, and learn your own lessons.

But hopefully this book has inspired you to think about doing things your own way

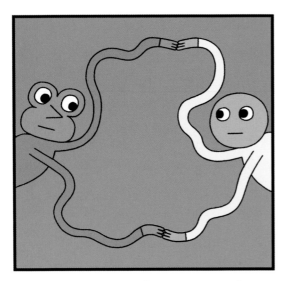

so you can be prepared for mess, or avoid it

and build relationships that work for you.

The relationship between
a book and its reader
is a beautiful thing.

A book doesn't really
have any meaning

until it is understood
by someone.

Hopefully, these pages

have made you feel
understood, too.

ABOUT THE AUTHOR

Hello, I am Alex Norris. I am from Swansea in Wales in the UK.

I make the webcomic *Webcomic Name*, where every comic ends with "oh no."

this is an example of a comic

they always end the same way

oh no

How to Love also began as a webcomic. Originally, it was a surreal parody of oversimplified love advice

and an excuse to hear about the love lives of everyone I know in the name of research.

Flies collide midair in a mating ritual called "striking"

this is very juicy gossip thank you

However, it soon became clear that readers were craving sincere advice, rooted in kindness and empathy.

I really relate to this character

I am a queer person, so this book is from a queer perspective, but I hope it is helpful to everyone.

my gayest hat

I'm not giving out advice because I think I have a perfect life.

why is my About the Author full of flies

I wanted to write a book that is intense and weird and silly. Just like me.

ACKNOWLEDGMENTS

I made this thing while I was going through a particularly difficult period of my life. I want to thank all of the incredible people who helped me through it, and also helped me make something I'm really proud of.

First of all, thank you to all the wonderful readers of the original *How to Love* series on Webtoon. Your insightful questions provided the basis for many of the chapters in this book.

Thank you to my beautiful family: Mum, Peter, Seb, and Gina. To my comics communities for your inspiration and kindness. And to my friends in Swansea, Bristol, London, and Margate for listening to me blather on about my ideas for so long, and telling me about your relationship joys and woes. I have crushes on many of you.

Thank you to Nicola Barr, Fran Perdomo, Kelly Roberts, Sarah Andersen, and Ruby Elliot for your help and support. Thank you to everyone at Walker, particularly Gráinne and Ben, for your patience and expertise, and your enthusiasm for my weird ideas.

To Ruby, my friend/lover/housemate, thank you for bringing joy and love into my life every day. It is extremely fun building a relationship with you.

And thank you to everyone else I have ever dated, especially Rosie and Amelia, for teaching me that the best relationships are big friendships.